W9-DAX-741

WITHDRAWN

BUGGIES, BICYCLES &
IRON HORSES
Transportation in the 1800s

DAILY LIFE IN AMERICA IN THE 1800s

BUGGIES, BICYCLES & IRON HORSES
Transportation in the 1800s

by
Kenneth McIntosh

Mason Crest Publishers

MASON CREST PUBLISHERS INC.
370 Reed Road
Broomall, Pennsylvania 19008
(866)MCP-BOOK (toll free)
www.masoncrest.com

First Printing
9 8 7 6 5 4 3 2 1

Library of Congress Cataloging-in-Publication Data

McIntosh, Kenneth, 1959-
  Buggies, bicycles and iron horses : transportation in the 1800s / by Kenneth R. McIntosh.
      p. cm. (Daily life in America in the 1800s)
  Includes bibliographical references and index.
  ISBN 978-1-4222-1776-4 (hardcover)   ISBN (series) 978-1-4222-1774-0
  ISBN 978-1-4222-1849-5 (pbk.)   ISBN (pbk series) 978-1-4222-1847-1
  1. Transportation—United States—History—19th century—Juvenile literature. I. Title.
  HE203.M335 2011
  388.30973'09034—dc22
                                    2010015443
Produced by Harding House Publishing Service, Inc.
www.hardinghousepages.com
Interior Design by MK Bassett-Harvey.
Cover design by Torque Advertising + Design.
Printed in USA by Bang Printing.

Contents

Introduction

History can too often seem a parade of distant figures whose lives have no connection to our own. It need not be this way, for if we explore the history of the games people play, the food they eat, the ways they transport themselves, how they worship and go to war—activities common to all generations—we close the gap between past and present. Since the 1960s, historians have learned vast amounts about daily life in earlier periods. This superb series brings us the fruits of that research, thereby making meaningful the lives of those who have gone before.

The authors' vivid, fascinating descriptions invite young readers to journey into a past that is simultaneously strange and familiar. The 1800s were different, but, because they experienced the beginnings of the same baffling modernity were are still dealing with today, they are also similar. This was the moment when millennia of agrarian existence gave way to a new urban, industrial era. Many of the things we take for granted, such as speed of transportation and communication, bewildered those who were the first to behold the steam train and the telegraph. Young readers will be interested to learn that growing up then was no less confusing and difficult then than it is now, that people were no more in agreement on matters of religion, marriage, and family then than they are now.

We are still working through the problems of modernity, such as environmental degradation, that people in the nineteenth century experienced for the first time. Because they met the challenges with admirable ingenuity, we can learn much from them. They left behind a treasure trove of alternative living arrangements, cultures, entertainments, technologies, even diets that are even more relevant today. Students cannot help but be intrigued, not just by the technological ingenuity of those times, but by the courage of people who forged new frontiers, experimented with ideas and social arrangements. They will be surprised by the degree to which young people were engaged in the great events of the time, and how women joined men in the great adventures of the day.

When history is viewed, as it is here, from the bottom up, it becomes clear just how much modern America owes to the genius of ordinary people, to the labor of slaves and immigrants, to women as well as men, to both young people and adults. Focused on home and family life, books in this series provide insight into how much of history is made within the intimate spaces of private life rather than in the remote precincts of public power. The 1800s were the era of the self-made man and women, but also of the self-made communities. The past offers us a plethora of heroes and heroines together with examples of extraordinary collective action from the Underground Railway to the creation of the American trade union movement. There is scarcely an immigrant or ethic organization in America today that does not trace its origins to the nineteenth century.

This series is exceptionally well illustrated. Students will be fascinated by the images of both rural and urban life; and they will be able to find people their own age in these marvelous depictions of play as well as work. History is best when it engages our imagination, draws us out of our own time into another era, allowing us to return to the present with new perspectives on ourselves. My first engagement with the history of daily life came in sixth grade when my teacher, Mrs. Polster, had us do special projects on the history of the nearby Erie Canal. For the first time, history became real to me. It has remained my passion and my compass ever since.

The value of this series is that it opens up a dialogue with a past that is by no means dead and gone but lives on in every dimension of our daily lives. When history texts focus exclusively on political events, they invariably produce a sense of distance. This series creates the opposite effect by encouraging students to see themselves in the flow of history. In revealing the degree to which people in the past made their own history, students are encouraged to imagine themselves as being history-makers in their own right. The realization that history is not something apart from ourselves, a parade that passes us by, but rather an ongoing pageant in which we are all participants, is both exhilarating and liberating, one that connects our present not just with the past but also to a future we are responsible for shaping.

—*Dr. John Gillis, Rutgers University Professor of History Emeritus*

Part I
Hoofin' It
THE ERA OF MUSCLE POWER

1800

1800 The Library of Congress is established.

1801

1801 Thomas Jefferson is elected as the third President of the United States.

1801 Richard Trevithick invents the first steam-powered locomotive, nicknamed "The Puffing Devil." It is designed for roads.

1803

1803 Louisiana Purchase—The United States purchases land from France and begins westward exploration.

1812

1812 War of 1812—Fought between the United States and the United Kingdom

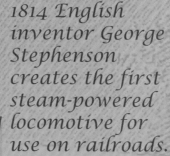

1814

1814 English inventor George Stephenson creates the first steam-powered locomotive for use on railroads.

1820

1820 Missouri Compromise—Agreement passes between pro-slavery and abolitionist groups, stating that all the Louisiana Purchase territory north of the southern boundary of Missouri (except for Missouri) will be free states, and the territory south of that line will be slave.

1804

1807

1804 Journey of Lewis and Clark—Lewis and Clark lead a team of explorers westward to the Columbia River in Oregon.

1807 Swiss inventor Isaac de Rivas creates a hydrogen gas-powered engine.

1807 Robert Fulton creates the first commercial steamboat (called the Clermont). The Clermont carries passengers from New York City to Albany, New York.

of the 1800s

1823

1825

1823 Monroe Doctrine—States that any efforts made by Europe to colonize or interfere with land owned by the United States will be viewed as aggression and require military intervention.

1825 The Erie Canal is completed— This allows direct transportation between the Great Lakes and the Atlantic Ocean.

On a typical day, you ride the bus to school, or one of your parents drives you in the car. When your family wants to travel, they pile into an SUV or buy an airplane ticket. We are accustomed to cheap, fast transportation. We take it for granted.

In 1841, Massachusetts philosopher Ralph Waldo Emerson wrote, "The civilized man has built a coach, but has lost the use of his feet." When he said this, most people thought of transportation in terms of muscle power—either that of humans or horses. Well-to-do folks could enjoy the comfort of a coach or wagon, but they still relied on the steed pulling it. Most of the world moved by foot or by hoof, and it moved very slowly over rough and dusty trails.

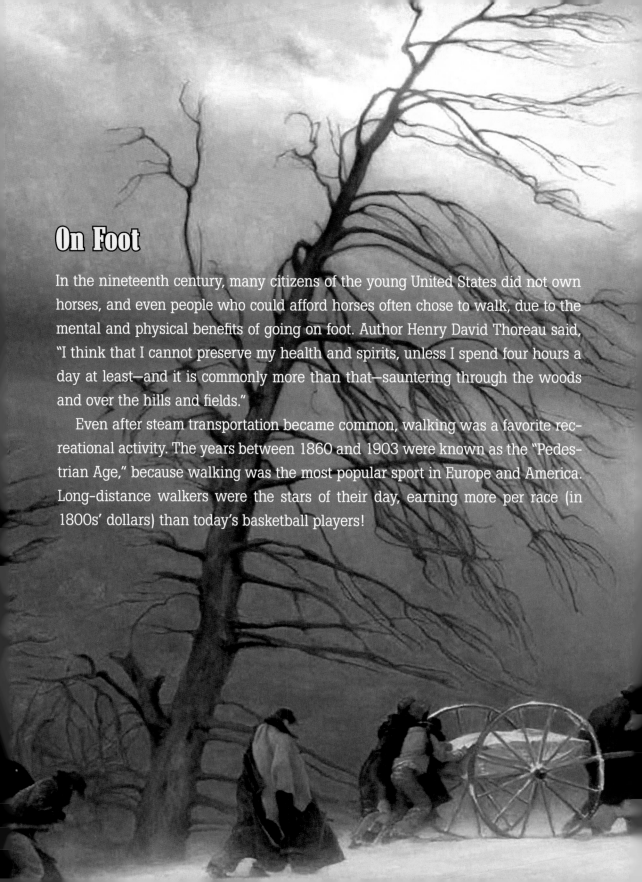

On Foot

In the nineteenth century, many citizens of the young United States did not own horses, and even people who could afford horses often chose to walk, due to the mental and physical benefits of going on foot. Author Henry David Thoreau said, "I think that I cannot preserve my health and spirits, unless I spend four hours a day at least—and it is commonly more than that—sauntering through the woods and over the hills and fields."

Even after steam transportation became common, walking was a favorite recreational activity. The years between 1860 and 1903 were known as the "Pedestrian Age," because walking was the most popular sport in Europe and America. Long-distance walkers were the stars of their day, earning more per race (in 1800s' dollars) than today's basketball players!

Walking West!

Western movies almost always portray pioneers heading west, riding in their horse-drawn or oxen-drawn covered wagons, and in fact, that is how many settlers headed to the new frontier—but not all. Some crossed the country on foot. If you had moved west in the 1800s, you could have purchased a walking ticket for your travel. This ticket allowed you to walk along with the wagon train.

Some pioneers walked west while pulling their belongings in handcarts. In the summer of 1856, members of the Church of Jesus Christ Latter Day Saints (Mormons) arrived in Iowa City; that was as far west as the train went in 1856. They were immigrants who had recently come to America from England and Wales, and they were determined to join their fellow believers in Utah. Lacking horses, they made handcarts, rickety two-wheeled devices similar to ox-carts but pulled by human power. Settlers pulled one handcart for every five persons, loaded with food, bedding, and clothing. Between 1856 and 1860, more than 3,000 Latter Day "saints" moved to their new home in Utah by pulling handcarts over rough and dangerous land.

Horse Power

An anonymous author coined the phrase, "The horse—man's noblest companion." But there were no horses in the Americas until Spanish settlers introduced Arabian steeds to the continent. Hernando Cortes described his victory over Native Aztecs, saying, "After God, we owed the victory to the horses."

Some of those Spanish horses escaped and multiplied in the American West. Native people, accustomed to using dogs as pack animals, were delighted with these new beasts—and quickly mastered the arts of horsemanship. Anglo Americans marveled at the "oneness" between Native warriors and their mounts.

At the same time, on farms and settlements in the East, Anglo Americans relied on draft horses: strong, tall beasts bred for heavy labor. These obedient and uncomplaining creatures enabled rural Americans to earn their

living, raise their food, and travel, until automobiles were invented.

Carriages and Buggies

As the United States grew, horse paths turned into roads. Horse-drawn carts required wider paths; and once people had made cart-paths, then they started using carriages or coaches. Carriages were wheeled compartments with springs holding the wheels, a design feature that made travel more comfortable than horseback or cart. Elegant carriages were status symbols, especially among Southern tobacco farmers.

At the start of the 1800s, use of carriages and wagons was at an all time high. Buggies—lightweight one-horse carriages, often with open tops—were also popular. Although riding in these vehicles was faster than travel by foot, they were not up to modern standards of comfort: rutted and rock-strewn roads rattled travelers' bones and sometimes broke carriage wheels.

Prairie Schooners

From the 1850s until the railroad was built across the country, covered wagons carried thousands of Americans to travel from the East to the new territories in the West. Promoters advertised new territories—such as Oregon—as "the loveliest country on earth," but upon their arrival after a long, challenging journey, settlers were often disappointed by the hardship of their new lives.

Oxen often pulled the covered wagons, and since oxen were ill suited to reins, the driver had to walk beside the beasts and goad them along—from the Mississippi River all the way to California or Oregon. Loaded goods took up most of the space inside the wagons, leaving room for only a few passengers, typically the elderly, young children, or folks who were suffering from illness. The passengers didn't have it much easier than the walkers, though: jarring bumps and dust from other wagons bothered travelers who rode inside these vehicles. Healthy pioneers—

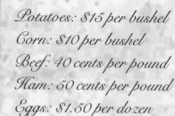

SETTLERS' SHOPPING LIST

If you were heading west, here's what you could have expected to pay for supplies in Denver. These prices were considered to be outrageous!

Potatoes: $15 per bushel
Corn: $10 per bushel
Beef: 40 cents per pound
Ham: 50 cents per pound
Eggs: $1.50 per dozen
Hay: $100 per ton
Wood: $75 per cord
Lumber: $200 per thousand
Wagon and team: $25 per day

including women, older children, and teens—walked alongside or behind the wagons.

People sometimes called these wagons "prairie schooners," a name that compared them to swift-moving sailing ships, but it wasn't a very good comparison: the so-called prairie schooners traveled at the speed of only two miles per hour. On average, it took six months to travel the 2,000-mile Oregon Trail—and the trek was hazardous.

Western films portray attacks by Natives or bandits, but wagon train travelers more often died from less romantic afflictions. Mishaps often occurred: settlers were crushed under moving wagon wheels, thrown by horses, trampled in stampedes, burned in grassfires, or injured in hailstorms. The worst nightmare was when hunger or heat brought down the horses or oxen; with no way to pull the wagon, a family faced likely death.

A restored covered wagon at Fort Bridger in Wyoming.

INCREDIBLE INDIVIDUAL
Jim Bridger

When he was only seventeen years old, Jim Bridger joined a group of Mountain Men (fur trappers) who were the first white men to behold the wonders of Yellowstone. In 1830, he and partners established the Rocky Mountain Fur Company, providing beaver pelts to be made into hats back East. Then in 1843, when the prairie schooners started heading for Oregon, he established Fort Bridger as a supply station and safe haven for the settlers. Shortly after that, he found Bridger's Pass—a shortcut that shaved three days of travel off the Oregon Trail. Later, the route Bridger established became the path of the first transcontinental railroad. In the 1860s, Bridger served as a guide and scout in conflicts between the government and Native Americans.

Bridger liked to tell tall tales, and half the time, people didn't know if he was telling the truth or stretching it. He fascinated settlers with his accounts of tall geysers that shot water and steam into the air, and a "peetrified forest" of logs turned to stone. These things seemed too incredible to believe until the pioneers saw them with their own eyes.

Pedal Pushers

In 1839, a Scotsman, Kirkpatrick Mac-Millan, is thought to have invented something that revolutionized muscle-powered transportation—the bicycle! The first bicycles (called velocipedes) had wooden frames and wooden wheels, with no suspension; pedals attached directly to the front wheel. Critics came up with an unkind name for these early bicycles: bone crushers. An American, Dr. William H. Laubach, of Philadelphia, made slight improvements on the velocipede design, and in 1869, he achieved the unimaginable speed of twenty miles an hour!

Around 1870, bicycle manufacturers introduced the all-metal high-wheeler with rubber tires, a great improvement over the velocipedes. These were much faster and more comfortable, so they became immensely popular. The disad-vantage to the new high-wheel design was safety: if anything got in the way of the front wheel—a rock, a stray dog, or a rut in the road—that sudden blockage resulted in what was known as "taking a header," a sudden painful dive over the front of the bicycle onto the road.

Velocipedes went through many shapes and sizes as they evolved into the modern bicycle.

VELOCIPEDE.

6. Renn-Bicycle „Invincible".

13. Humber-Tricycle.

10. Manuped.

12. Sicherheits-Bicycle „Rover".

8. Saal-Bicycle.

11. Reitmaschine nach Freiherrn von Drais.

2. Tandem-Tricycle von Humber u. Comp.

3. Touren-Bicycle „Leipzig".

1. Touren-Tricycle „Invincible".

5. „Sociable" für 2 Personen, verwandelbar in ein Tricycle.

7. Gepäck-Transport-Dreirad.

9. Otto-Bicycle.

4. Monocycle.

14. Renn-Tandem-Tricycle „Invincible".

Bloomers allowed women to ride bicycles more safely and modestly, but many more conservative people felt that they indicated an immoral trend. According to the Syracuse Post, "a woman who wears bloomers has loose habits."

Finally, in 1888, veterinarian John Dunlop patented the pneumatic (air-filled) tire, and applied this invention to the "safety" design bicycle, resulting in bicycles virtually identical to some used today. Throughout the nineteenth-century's "gay nineties," bicycles were a popular and efficient means of transportation for the average American. They were so popular that ladies started wearing "bloomers"—the first pants designed for women.

In 1892, English composer Harry Dacre moved to America, bringing his bicycle with him. Shortly after his arrival, he penned one of the most popular songs of the late 1800s, titled "Daisy":

> *Daisy, Daisy, give me your answer, do,*
> *I'm half crazy all for the love of you.*
> *It won't be a stylish marriage—*
> *I can't afford a carriage,*
> *But you'd look sweet upon the seat*
> *Of a bicycle built for two.*

An 1886 bicycle built for two.

EYEWITNESS ACCOUNT

Wagons West

(Edward H. N. Patterson traveled by wagon train from Illinois to California for the Gold Rush, in 1850.)

Thursday, March 28

Left camp this morning in good season and travelled over a beautiful road passing through Winchester, Birmingham and Libertyville. After we left Libertyville we were deceived by a "cut-off" and leaving the main road we found ourselves in for it—completely taken in and done for. The road for eight miles was awful—hills, hollows, mud holes, wet prairie, bad bridges—everything that could render a road execrable. I hope the boys didn't curse it much but for my own part, I was much in the mood of old Deacon, whose hat flew off—"It's against my profession to swear, but, neighbor, you will greatly oblige me by damning that hat."

EXTRA! EXTRA! GOLD RUSH!

The California Star
Saturday, June 10, 1848

Every seaport as far south as San Diego, and every interior town, and nearly every rancho from the base of the mountains, in which the gold has been found has become suddenly drained of human beings. Americans, Californians, Indians and Sandwich Islanders, men, women and children, indiscriminately. Should there be that success which has repaid the efforts of those employed for the last month, we confess to unhesitatingly believe probably, not only will witness the depopulation of every town, the desertion of every rancho, and the desolation of the once promising crops of the country, but it will also draw largely upon adjacent territories—awake Sonora, and call down upon us, despite her Indian battles, a great many of the good people of Oregon. There are at this time over one thousand souls busied in washing gold, and the yield per diem may be safely estimated at from fifteen to twenty dollars, each individual.

PONY EXPRESS
St. JOSEPH, MISSOURI to CALIFORNIA
in 10 days or less.

YOUNG, SKINNY, WIRY FELLOWS
not over eighteen. Must be expert
riders, willing to risk death daily.
Orphans preferred.
Wages $25 per week.

APPLY, **PONY EXPRESS STABLES**
St. JOSEPH, MISSOURI

Jason Balfry felt light as the wind and so full of pride he thought for sure his heart would bust out his chest with happiness. At sixteen, he had never dreamed of such an adventure. It had been a long shot when he answered the posted advertisement for "brave young men, skilled with horse and pistol, able to ride swiftly" who "must provide own horse, fast and healthy" in order to "deliver mail safely and reliably across the wilderness." He was thrilled when a company officer came to his house to offer him the job, and even more excited when

An actual poster advertising for Pony Express riders like Jason.

his widowed mother agreed to let him take the work, saying, "It's dangerous but we can sure use the money." So now, Jason rode one lap in a relay across the frontier, from Missouri to California—the fastest way to deliver mail from one side of the country to the other.

He spurred his appaloosa, Charlie, on to a gallop as they entered a slot canyon. Suddenly, Charlie reared up, whinnying. Jason held on tight to the reigns. "Hey! Whatcha stopping for?" Then Jason saw.

Ahead on the trail, four Apache warriors blocked their way, each astride fine-looking mounts, each armed with shields, lances, or bows. Jason wheeled Charlie around to beat a fast retreat, but then his heart sank: three more warriors blocked the way back. He was surrounded.

One of the group of four rode closer to Jason; this warrior was maybe thirty years of age with long black hair and a cougar-skin cap, topped with owl feathers. The warrior addressed Jason in English. "What are you doing here, young man? Why are you going so fast?"

"I—I'm with the Pony Express. I'm carrying mail."

The warrior cocked an eyebrow, and Jason reached down into one of the leather saddlebags, producing a sealed letter.

The warrior nodded. "Talking pouches—I have seen white people get those. You are not bringing settlers—no wagons follow you?"

"No, sir." Jason shook his head. "Just mail . . . and I have to come through here every couple days."

The Apache's stern face broke into a grin. "I'm Swift Owl." He gestured around him. "These are our lands. As long as you do not bring more white men, then you can travel through here under my protection." He broke a feather off his cap and handed it to Jason. "Keep this tied to your shirt. It is the sign of my promise." Swift Owl motioned to his companions, and they took off at a gallop.

Jason gave sigh of relief and leaned over to pat Charlie's neck. "We lucked out that time, old boy. Looks like we have some new friends."

Part II
Canoes, Clippers, and
River Queens

1838

1838 Trail of Tears—General Winfield Scott and 7,000 troops force Cherokees to walk from Georgia to a reservation set up for them in Oklahoma (nearly 1,000 miles). Around 4,000 Native Americans die during the journey.

1839

1839 The first camera is patented by Louis Daguerre.

1839 Scotsman Kirkpatrick MacMillan is thought to have invented the first bicycle (called a velocipede).

1840

1840 The world's first cable car system opens in London, England.

Time Line

1854

1854 Kansas-Nebraska Act—States that each new state entering the country will decide for themselves whether or not to allow slavery. This goes directly against the terms agreed upon in the Missouri Compromise of 1820.

The Lenoir Gas Engine

1859

1859 John Brown's Rebellion—John Brown leads a revolt and takes over the federal arsenal at Harper's Ferry, Virginia. However, he is soon forced to surrender by U.S. marines, and then is hung for his crimes.

1859 Belgian engineer Jean Joseph Étienne Lenoir creates the first engine that runs on gasoline.

1844

1844 First public telegraph line in the world is opened—between Baltimore and Washington.

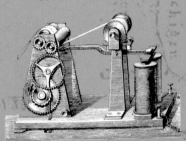

1848

1848 Seneca Falls Convention—Feminist convention held for women's suffrage and equal legal rights.

1848(-58) California Gold Rush—Over 300,000 people flock to California in search of gold.

1853

1853 British engineer George Cayley first shows his glider in flight. It is the first airborne vehicle in the world.

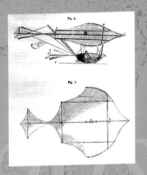

of the 1800s

1860

1860 The Pony Express begins delivering mail across the Great Plains and Rocky Mountains to the West.

1861

1861(-65) Civil War—Fought between the Union and Confederate states.

1862

1862 Emancipation Proclamation—Lincoln states that all slaves in Union states are to be freed.

Modern travelers sometimes complain about potholes in the roads, but most of us can hardly imagine the awful conditions of overland travel in the early 1800s. Roads for carriages and horses were little more than glorified dirt pathways, deeply rutted and worn, bumpy with rocks and even small boulders. Carriages and wagons often literally fell apart, and travelers arrived with their bones shaken and aching from the jarring roads.

The calmest and quickest way to move freight was by water. From the start of the nineteenth century until railroads became common, a great assortment of boats, rafts, and ships constantly floated up and down America's waterways, delivering goods, people, and animals.

The canoe was the oldest and cheapest method of water transportation. When Europeans arrived on North America's east coast, they found Natives gliding up and down the rivers in canoes made from tree bark sewn onto wooden frames, with upturned prow and stern. This style of canoe is so efficient that similar boats made with modern materials are often used today. For the first half of the nineteenth century, Natives, trappers, and hunters continued to use these vessels throughout the Midwest.

that every Native coast-dweller could have been afloat at any given time. First Nations people of the Northwest made these vessels between forty and sixty feet long, and used them for travel, ceremonies, fishing, and whaling. With sails, these seaworthy canoes could travel as far as 150 miles a day.

When Lewis and Clark started up the Missouri River in 1804, they were the first official explorers for the U.S. government, but traders had used that river for a highway long before their expedition. French voyageurs (traders) paddled dugout canoes loaded with knives, glass beads, and rum—goods they traded to Natives for beaver pelts.

Native tribes on the Pacific Coast of America, from Central California up to British Columbia, made sea-going canoes from cedar planks. In the mid-nineteenth centuries, about 10,000 of these canoes were on the sea, enough

HOW MUCH DID IT COST TO TRAVEL IN THE 1800S?

overnight lodging: 25 cents to $2.00 (depending on how fancy the accommodations)
train ticket: $1.00
cost of a meal on a train: 75 cents
cost of a bicycle: $135

PUT THINGS IN PERSPECTIVE

The average income during the 1800s was about $400 a year—or about $1.25 a day.

Canals: The First Super Highways

In 1810, a dreamer named Elkanah Watson proposed construction of an enormous ditch 362 miles long, connecting the Hudson River to Lake Erie. Thomas Jefferson thought it was "little short of madness," but work began, with Irish immigrants constructing a water route 40 feet wide and 4 feet deep, including seventy-two locks (water gates) that raised water 500 feet over the length of the canal.

When workers completed the Erie Canal in 1825, it quickly became the most popular way to travel that portion of the country.

Horses or mules pulled the canal boats, towing them from paths beside the canal. On average, canal boats traveled a mile and a half an hour. This doesn't seem very fast by modern standards, but the canal cut in half the price of freight going west.

Clipper Ships Connect the World

The mid-1800s brought new and exciting opportunities for global trade. The Gold Rush in California created demand for a fast way to get to the West Coast, and the potato famine in Ireland raised demand for transportation of immigrants to America. The Orient had long been closed to the West, but in 1853, Commodore Matthew Perry sailed four U.S. Navy warships into Tokyo Bay and forced the Japanese government to accept international trade. China and Japan had two important products that Americans wanted: the "proper" product was tea, and the more dangerous product was opium (a drug made from poppies). Even before these developments, new markets were opening up for products from Africa and India. All these demands required a new style of ship, one that could quickly transport cargo across the oceans.

In 1832, Isaac McKim, a wealthy Baltimore merchant, hired shipbuilders to construct the ship of his dreams, a vessel that weighed more than 500 tons, with three masts and stacks of square sails but with a narrow lightweight hull built for speed. Sailors and traders laughed at McKim's "fool ideas" for a new kind of ship and predicted disaster for the vessel, but

A poster advertising a "package deal" for passage to the Gold Rush, plus mules once you got there.

they were soon proved wrong. Named the *Ann McKim* after Isaac's beloved wife, she was the first clipper ship, a design that would rule the waves for the next forty years. Builders around the world immediately began copying the lines of the *Ann McKim*, and these clippers set records for speedy voyages to California's gold fields and to China's far away shores.

New England clipper ships were fast and beautiful, but their glory days lasted only a few decades. When the first clipper was built, someone had already invented a form of technology that would replace it—the steam ship.

A clipper ship.

Paddle Wheels and River Queens

In 1769, Scotsman James Watt patented the steam engine, ushering in the Industrial Revolution. Eighteen years later, American inventor John Fitch made the first successful run of a steam-propelled boat, with its boiler pushing six paddles down the Delaware River. Then, in 1807, Robert Fulton's Clermont went from New York City to Albany, making history with a 150-mile trip that took thirty-two hours at an average speed of 5 miles per hour. Fulton's Clermont, with a pair of paddle wheels, one on each side of the boat, was the first practical design for a steam ship.

Early steamboats were dangerous contraptions; female passengers rode in smaller boats towed behind, so they would be safe if the boiler exploded.

In 1811, Robert Fulton built *The New Orleans*, the first steamboat to travel up and down the Mississippi River. The idea caught on quickly, so much so that by 1834, Mississippi steamers were built at the rate of 1,200 per year, and by 1850, the number increased to 3,000 per year. These "sternwheeler" or "river queen" steamboats were very fancy, with their grand staircases, carpeted lounges, and luxurious pas-

John Fitch's steam-propelled boat.

senger cabins. Professional gamblers and fashionable travelers laughed and flirted in their floating saloons. The boats weren't exactly safe, however: in thirty-nine years, there were 44 collisions, 166 fires, 209 boiler explosions, and 576 steamboats sank from hitting obstacles in the water.

Free blacks and slaves often worked side by side on the Mississippi steamers. It was hard and dangerous work, but there was one advantage to these jobs: work on the river, with frequent stops at many locations, provided slaves with opportunities to escape and then find employment as free persons.

A Mississippi steamboat.

INCREDIBLE INDIVIDUAL
Robert Fulton

Fulton was born in Little Britain, Pennsylvania, in 1765. As a child, he enjoyed building mechanical toys, including a rocket and a paddle wheel boat. In 1786, Fulton left the United States to pursue a painting career in England. This didn't go well, so in 1797, he moved to France, hoping to sell his newly invented submarine to the French. In 1800, Fulton launched his first submarine, the Nautilus, at Rouen. It worked—descended 24 feet and came up again safely—but it was not practical for military use, so Fulton moved back to the United States and pursued his interest in steamboats. In 1807, Fulton launched the Clermont, a steamboat that traveled at a speed of nearly 5 miles per hour. Over the following years, Fulton created thirteen more steamboats, and lived to see his design transform transportation in America.

EYEWITNESS ACCOUNT

From *Life on the Mississippi*
by Mark Twain

In the "flush times" of steamboating, a race between two notoriously fleet steamers was an event of vast importance. The date was set for it several weeks in advance, and from that time forward, the whole Mississippi Valley was in a state of consuming excitement. Politics and the weather were dropped, and people talked only of the coming race. As the time approached, the two steamers "stripped" and got ready. . . .

The chosen date being come, and all things in readiness, the two great steamers back into the stream, and lie there jockeying a moment, and apparently watching each other's slightest movement, like sentient creatures; flags drooping, the pent steam shrieking through safety-valves, the black smoke rolling and tumbling from the chimneys and darkening all the air. People, people everywhere; the shores, the house-tops, the steamboats, the ships, are packed with them, and you know that the borders of the broad Mississippi are going to be fringed with humanity thence northward twelve hundred miles, to welcome these racers.

Presently tall columns of steam burst from the 'scape-pipes of both steamers, two guns boom a good-by, two red-shirted heroes mounted on capstans wave their small flags above the massed crews on the forecastles, two plaintive solos linger on the air a few waiting seconds, two mighty choruses burst forth—and here they come! Brass bands bray Hail Columbia, huzza after huzza thunders from the shores, and the stately creatures go whistling by like the wind.

(Mark Twain worked on a steamboat as a young man and published his memories in the book titled Life on the Mississippi; it was the first book entirely produced on a typewriter.)

EXTRA! EXTRA! *LUCY WALKER* STEAMBOAT EXPLODES!

The Sun, Baltimore, Maryland,
31 October 1844

It is by a miraculous dispensation of Divine Providence that I am enabled to write you a few lines. I have but a few hours ago escaped from the very jaws of Death. I arrived at Louisville last night and took passage in the steamboat "Lucy Walker", for New Orleans, that left at 12 o'clock to-day. We had proceeded but 5 or 6 miles below this place, when she burst her boilers, causing one of the most terrible explosions ever known, scattering death and havoc all around.

As it is, scarcely twenty survive, of a vast number of passengers. The scene beggars description; ladies crying for their lost husbands and children, and men rendered frantic by their scalds and wounds. I escaped without a bruise or a scar of the slightest kind, though I have lost all my clothing and baggage, besides valuable evidences of debt and important papers in my trunk. I am even without a hat, and merely saved the clothes I have on. I am now in the house of a Mr. Smith, of this place, who has kindly furnished me with a suit of clothes until mine dries. The people of this place have been very kind to the sufferers, five of whom have died since they came on shore. I should suppose that at least forty of the cabin passengers were either killed or wounded. All those standing around me on the hurricane deck, when I left it, are killed.

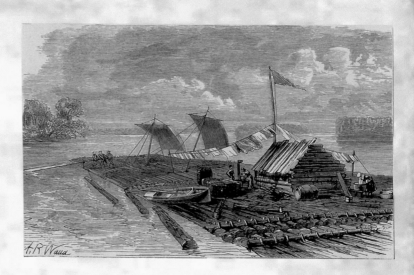

Jimmy Bartlett sweated and pulled at the oar, second-guessing his flight from home. He had grown tired of the boredom of farm work in Ohio and angered by his father's constant drunkenness and bad temper. After his mother died, the beatings got worse, so one night Jimmy slipped out, took a horse, and galloped deeper into the frontier. Then he took a job working for the American Fur Company. For the most part, it was exciting. His companions were all a bit crazy, but over time he came to enjoy their carefree spirits. He learned to trap and hunt, to throw a tomahawk and build a fire and lean-to. He met Natives with strange customs and he was fascinated by their way of life.

But now, the trappers were returning with several tons of pelts, loaded in a pile in the middle of the enormous raft they called a "Mackinaw." The huge boat was unwieldy; six men, all bigger than Jimmy was, could barely keep the vessel on course, although they pulled and cussed at the oars with all their might.

Jimmy thought to himself, I still don't want to go home. At least he was his own man here, and even the most abusive treatment from his fellow trappers fell short of what he had suffered at his father's hand. Still, this was painful hard work. Maybe he'd look for some other job when they got to town.

Snapshot from the Past

Aboard a Ship from Ireland to America,
Somewhere in the Atlantic, 1851

Maire O'Neil was asleep, having nightmares, when a sudden strong pitch of the ship woke her to the living nightmare in the gloomy hold of the English ship "William of Orange," bound for the New World with 107 men, women, and children jammed below decks. (At least that had been the number at departure; Maire was uncertain how many passengers had since died and been cast overboard.) She was wedged against a bulkhead, pressed in with her two sisters,

her brother, and her mother and father. Around them, the other passengers were stuffed so tight they could barely move.

A sharp ache cut into her stomach like a knife, a constant reminder that she was starving. Her family hadn't realized they were supposed to provide their own food for the voyage until they were already underway—but even had they known, they would have had no food to bring. They were half-starving already before they left.

When the children whimpered, Mother and Father reminded them, "We had no future at home. America is the land of opportunity. You'll see, our fortunes will change as soon as we leave this ship."

Maire hoped they were right.

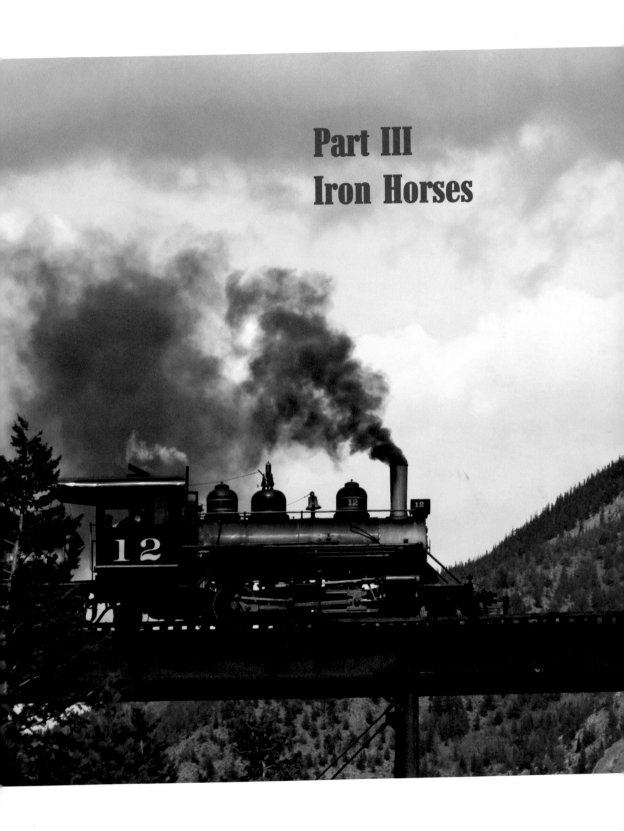

Part III
Iron Horses

1865

1865 Thirteenth Amendment to the United States Constitution—Officially abolishes slavery across the country.

1865 President Abraham Lincoln is assassinated on April 15.

1867

1867 United States purchases Alaska from Russia.

1867 Sylvester Howard Roper shows his steam-powered velocipede, the very first motorcycle ever created, at fairs and circuses on the East Coast of the United States.

1869

1869 Transcontinental Railroad completed on May 10.

Time Line

1885

1885 German Karl Benz invents the first truly self-powered automobile, patenting it as the Benz Patent Motorwagen.

1886

1886 The Statue of Liberty is dedicated on October 28.

1890

1890 Wounded Knee Massacre—Last battle in the American Indian Wars.

1892

1892 Ellis Island is opened to receive immigrants coming into New York.

1870 Fifteenth Amendment to the United States Constitution—Prohibits any citizen from being denied to vote based on their "race, color, or previous condition of servitude."

1870 Christmas is declared a national holiday.

1876 Alexander Graham Bell invents the telephone.

1877 Great Railroad Strike—Often considered the country's first nationwide labor strike.

1878 Thomas Edison patents the phonograph on February 19.

1878 Thomas Edison invents the light bulb on October 22.

of the 1800s

1896   1898   1899

1896 Plessy vs. Ferguson—Supreme Court case that rules that racial segregation is legal as long as accommodations are kept equal.

1896 Henry Ford builds his first combustion-powered vehicle, which he names the Ford Quadricycle.

1898 The Spanish-American War—The United States gains control of Cuba, Puerto Rico, and the Philippines.

1899 Ferdinand von Zeppelin patents the Zeppelin, the first airship (also known as a dirigible).

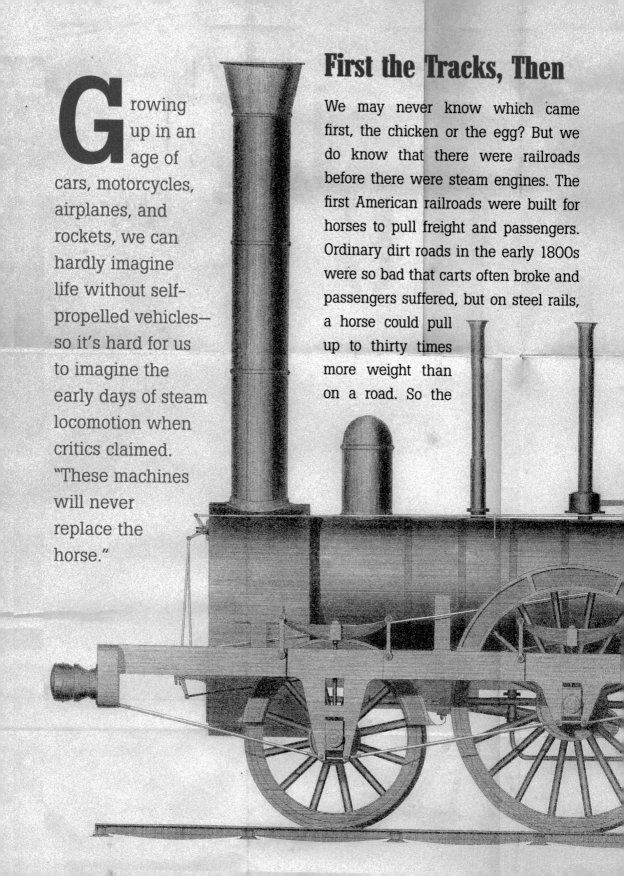

Growing up in an age of cars, motorcycles, airplanes, and rockets, we can hardly imagine life without self-propelled vehicles—so it's hard for us to imagine the early days of steam locomotion when critics claimed. "These machines will never replace the horse."

First the Tracks, Then

We may never know which came first, the chicken or the egg? But we do know that there were railroads before there were steam engines. The first American railroads were built for horses to pull freight and passengers. Ordinary dirt roads in the early 1800s were so bad that carts often broke and passengers suffered, but on steel rails, a horse could pull up to thirty times more weight than on a road. So the

the Train

Baltimore and Ohio Railroad was built in 1827, covering 379 miles, powered by horses.

Mr. Peter Cooper was an investor in that railroad and an inventor. Then he thought of a wild idea: the railroad would make more money if steam engines rather than horses powered it. The owners were doubtful because the first steam locomotive –invented five years earlier in England—was slow and unreliable. But Cooper was undaunted, and he began work on his own loco-motive. His design was entirely different from the British version: all the parts were smaller and lighter. He called his engine *The Tom Thumb*, named after the tiny folk hero who conquered giants. This first American steam locomotive had one and a half horsepower.

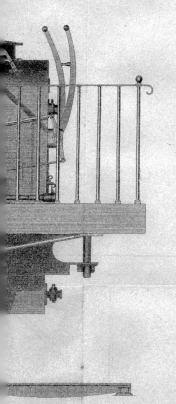

August 28, 1830 was a famous day of reckoning for American transportation. Peter Cooper, with his *Tom Thumb* steam engine, raced against a celebrated packhorse hitched to a carriage. They were both on railroad tracks, side by side. The horse and locomotive started out together as the crowd screamed and whistled; people had the feeling that the future was at stake. Then to Mr. Cooper's great disappointment, a belt connecting the engine to the wheels slipped off the *Tom Thumb*. He did a mid-race repair, but the horse won that competition. Spectators went home murmuring "They'll never replace the horse," but history was on the side of the steam locomotive.

Within the next few years, more than a dozen steam railroads sprang up, connecting all the major cities of the Eastern United States, and a decade

after Mr. Cooper's first steam engine, travelers could get from Boston to Buffalo by steam train. There was a hitch, though: none of the passenger lines went more than fifty miles in a single direction, so to make the trip from Massachusetts to Upstate New York, a traveler had to jump on and off eight different trains. Worst, none of the railway companies coordinated schedules, so the waits between trains could be very long. Yet with all these problems, railroads still moved more people further and faster than humans had ever traveled before. The future belonged to trains.

How the West Was Really Won

From the day that gold was discovered in California, Americans faced a frustrating problem: how could people travel conveniently from the settled Eastern states to the California coast? The overland journey meant months walking behind covered wagons on bone-breaking trails through deadly deserts. By clipper ship, it still took months to sail all the way down around South America and up again, braving often-dangerous weather. Visionaries

dreamed of a railroad line connecting coast to coast across the country. Critics scoffed. The *New York Herald* newspaper said such plans were "ridiculous and absurd. Centuries hence will be time to talk of such a railroad." Yet in 1862, the American government granted a charter for construction of the transcontinental rail line, and although the Civil War hindered progress, work began.

Designers chose to follow the stagecoach route of Ben Holliday's Overland Stages, and the Central Pacific Company started laying track from the East while the Union Pacific started from the West. After the war, these companies hired thousands of Chinese and Irish laborers, workers who endured dangerous conditions, rough weather, and very low wages. Sometimes they were close to dynamite explosions, other times they dangled over cliffs in baskets—but they got the job done. On May 10, 1869, Leland Stanford, President of the Central Pacific Company, drove in the final Golden Spike at Promontory, Utah, completing the transcontinental railroad. He missed on the first swing—but there were no video cameras to record the mistake, and onlookers quickly forgot that as they moved on to wild celebrations of their achievement.

In legends, the West was "tamed" by wagon-train settlers and heroic sheriffs. In reality, railroads brought civilization from coast to coast. Wherever the trains stopped, cities sprang up. Fred Harvey, entrepreneur, built a chain of fine restaurants and hotels across the country wherever the trains stopped; his "Harvey Girls" brought a new level of refinement and politeness to the rough-and-tumble frontier. Justice, peace, and prosperity came to the Wild West aboard the iron horses.

The joining of the rails at Promontory, Utah, on May 10, 1869. In the center, S. S. Montague (left) of the Central Pacific is shaking hands with Grenville M. Dodge (right) of the Union Pacific.

EXTRA! EXTRA! BUILDING THE TRANSCONTINENTAL RAILROAD

by Dr. William Abraham Bell,
1866

A light car, drawn by a single horse, gallops up to the front with its load of rails.

Two men seize the end of a rail and start forward, the rest of the gang taking hold by twos, until it is clear of the car. They come forward at a run. At the word of command the rail is dropped in its place, right side up with care, while the same process goes on at the other side of the car. Less than thirty seconds to a rail for each gang, and so four rails go down to the minute.

Close behind the first gang come the gaugers, spikers, and bolters, and a lively time they make of it. It is a grand "anvil chorus." It is played in triple time, 3 strokes to the spike. There are 10 spikes to a rail, 400 rails to a mile, 1,800 miles to San Francisco—21,000,000 times those sledges to be swung: 21,000,000 times are they to come down with their sharp punctuation before the great work of modern America is complete.

Glimpses of the Incredible Future

At the beginning of the nineteenth century, most Americans walked and the more fortunate rode horses. Decades later, citizens were awed at the amazing technology of steam-driven railroads and riverboats. By the end of the century, there were hopeful glimpses of an even greater miracle ahead—the horseless carriage.

Even before the Civil War, American inventors were trying to create practical steam cars. In 1871, Dr. J. W. Carhart of Wisconsin State University built a working steam car that inspired the State of Wisconsin, in 1878, to offer a $10,000 prize to the winner of a 200-mile race. Only two cars showed up at the starting line, and one car managed to finish the whole distance with an average speed of 6 miles per hour.

On September 21, 1893, in Springfield, Massachusetts, brothers Charles and Frank Duryea drove a carriage powered by a four-horsepower gasoline-fueled motor. This horseless carriage was still a long way from practical, but citizens of the United States caught their first glimpse of the world where you and I live today.

An early "steam carriage."

SNAPSHOT FROM THE PAST

The Horseless Carriage,
San Francisco, 1899.

Toby, come quick! You've gotta see this!"

Ten-year-old Toby raced out the door, and looked where his friend Charlie pointed up the curving street on which they both lived. At the top of the hill, a crowd was gathered around a strange-looking contraption: it was a real-by-golly horseless carriage!

The two boys ran up and pushed their way past the grownups to the front of the crowd. An elegant man with a mustache, wearing goggles and a long gray duster coat, stood atop the machine. "This motor produces an amazing three horse power," he explained. "That's right—the power of three magnificent steeds, contained in this tiny metal box." He motioned at an oily steel block in the back of the carriage. "There is no need for reins, I steer it by means of this

simple handle—like guiding a ship," and he pointed to a long bar connected to the front wheels then sweeping up over the seat.

"And now ladies and gentlemen, I shall demonstrate." He made a dramatic bow and stepped behind the carriage, where he gave a handle several hard cranks. The piston began to shoot back and forth with a loud poom-poom-poom noise, and white smelly smoke billowed out from a pipe behind the engine.

The inventor jumped into the seat of the carriage and pulled back on a bar, simultaneously grasping the steering handle. People jumped out of the way as the motor revved louder, and the horseless carriage sprang forward. It rattled down the cobblestones and turned a corner, beginning to descend the hill at a frightening speed.

Just then, a dog sprang onto the road, yapping at the strange contraption. The driver pulled quickly back on the accelerator lever, and the motor made a tremendous ka-bang, at the same instant that the front wheels turned abruptly sidewise and locked up. The horseless carriage flew off of the road and smashed into a flower-seller's stall, just as a panicked vendor jumped out of the way. The inventor picked himself up off the ground, dusting his jacket and shaking his head.

Toby heard the grownups around him muttering.

"What a disaster!"

"Get a horse!"

"They should outlaw these crazy contraptions. Someday someone is really gonna get hurt."

But Toby thought differently. "When I grow up," he said, "I'm gonna buy me a horseless carriage. Then I'll have the fastest thing on the road."

Think About It

The changes and improvements in transportation methods and networks during the 1800s changed America from a nation of East coast communities connected by mostly bad roads to one where transcontinental distances had been conquered by railroads and steamships crossed the Atlantic in a matter of days rather than weeks.

- How do you think the limits of transportation in 1800 affected the way a person your age would have viewed the world around him? What would have been his knowledge of people and places outside of his hometown?

- Which transportation innovation do you think caused the most change in Americans' way of life?

- As a young person of the twenty-first century, where both physical and cyberspace distances between people are getting smaller all the time, how is your worldview different from that of someone living in the 1800s? How much more do you think you might know about people outside your hometown? How big is your sense of "community"?

Words Used in This Book

boiler: The part of a steam engine where water is converted into steam.

entrepreneur: A person who is responsible for starting and managing a business.

execrable: Very bad.

famine: A time when there is not enough food to keep people alive and healthy.

First Nations: A term that refers to the native people who lived in the Americas when the Europeans arrived.

freight: Goods that are shipped from one place to another.

frontier: The region at the edge of settled territory.

global: Having to do with the entire world.

hull: The frame or body of a boat or ship.

Industrial Revolution: The period in European and North American history when power-driven machinery was introduced, bringing about major changes in the way people lived and worked.

locomotion: The act or power to move from place to place.

Natives: The first people to live in a place; in this book, "Natives" refers to the people already living in the Americas when Europeans arrived.

Orient: The Far East.

pelts: Animal skins.

prow: The front of a boat or ship.

revolutionized: Brought about a major change in the way something is done.

rural: Having to do with the country (vs. the city).

stern: The rear part of a boat or ship.

transcontinental: Having to do with crossing the continent.

visionaries: People who have big ideas for the future.

Find Out More

In Books

Bain, David Haward. *Empire Express: Building the First Transcontinental Railroad.* New York: Penguin, 2000.

Dooling, Michael. *The Great Horseless Carriage Race.* New York: Holiday House, 2002.

Fine, Jil. *The Transcontinental Railroad: Tracks Across America.* New York: Children's Press, 2005.

Foster, Genevieve. *The Year of the Horseless Carriage: 1801.* San Luis Obispo, Calif.: Beautiful Feet Books, 2008.

Koeppel, Gerard. *Bond of Union: Building the Erie Canal and the American Empire.* Cambridge, Mass.: De Capo, 2009.

On the Internet

1800s Transportation and Technology
www.northwesthistoryexpress.com/timeline/transportation1800.php

Transportation in the Nineteenth Century
history1800s.about.com/od/transportation/Transportation.htm

Travel and Transportation of the 1800s
houck.salkeiz.k12.or.us/cool.sites/ss/1800.travel/travel.1800.html

Index

Picture Credits

Church of Latter Day Saints 14–15

Creative Commons
    Georges Jansoone 44–45

Currier & Ives 39

Fort Bridger, Wyoming State Park 19–20

Library of Congress 12–13, 18, 22–24, 34, 40

Maryland Archives 37

Mississippi Historical Archives 29, 44–45

New York State Archives 35, 38

Pony Express Stables Museum, St. Joseph, Missouri 26–27

Rochester Historical Society 52–53

Smithsonian Museum 33

Texas Historical Archives 41

Yellowstone National Park, U.S. Dept. of the Interior 16–18

To the best knowledge of the publisher, all images not specifically credited are in the public domain. If any image has been inadvertently uncredited, please notify Harding House Publishing Service, 220 Front Street, Vestal, New York 13850, so that credit can be given in future printings.

About the Author and the Consultant

Kenneth McIntosh is the author of more than sixty books, including titles in the Mason Crest series North American Indians Today. He also teaches college classes. He and his wife live in Flagstaff, Arizona, a town with an abundance of heritage sites from the 1800s.

John Gillis is a Rutgers University Professor of History Emeritus. A graduate of Amherst College and Stanford University, he has taught at Stanford, Princeton, University of California at Berkeley, as well as Rutgers. Gillis is well known for his work in social history, including pioneering studies of age relations, marriage, and family. The author or editor of ten books, he has also been a fellow at both St. Antony's College, Oxford, and Clare Hall, Cambridge.